Life is too short to wake up in the morning with regrets. So, love the people who treat you right and forget about the ones who don't. Believe that everything happens for a reason. If you get a chance – take it; if it changes your life – let it.

Nobody said that it would be easy.

BUT

it would be worth it.

– Paulo Coelho

There is no failure, only feedback.
— *Robert Allen*

No one can make you feel inferior without your consent.
— *Eleanor Roosevelt*

'Tis better than riches to scratch where it itches.
   — Heather Baker

Happiness comes of the capacity to feel deeply, to enjoy simply,
to think freely, to risk life, to be needed.
— *Storm Jameson*

Innovation distinguishes between a reactive and a proactive Assistant.
— *Andrea Macarie*

What do we live for, if not to make life less difficult for each other?
— *George Elliot*

At the side of the everlasting why, there is a yes, and a yes, and a yes.
  – EM Forster

Don't be scared – live life to the fullest – Karma will do the rest.
– *Sherri Dawn*

Dream it – believe it – achieve it.
(Unknown)

Learning never exhausts the mind.
— *Leonardo da Vinci*

Once social change begins, it cannot be reversed. You cannot uneducate the person who has learned to read. You cannot humiliate the person who feels pride. You cannot oppress the people who are not afraid anymore.

We have seen the future and the future is ours.

– Cesar Chavez

Education is the most powerful weapon which you can use to change the world.
— *Nelson Mandela*

My friends are my estate.
   — Emily Dickenson

The best and most beautiful things in the world cannot be seen or even touched —
they must be felt with the heart.
— Hellen Keller

Nothing is impossible, the word itself says "I'm possible".
— *Audrey Hepburn*

Sometimes you can't see yourself clearly
until you see yourself through the eyes of others.
— *Ellen Degeneres*

Self-confidence is the best outfit. Rock it. Own it.
   — Debbi Shaffer

You become what you believe.
You are where you are today in life based on everything you have believed.
— Oprah Winfrey

When you learn how much you're worth, you'll stop giving people discounts.
— *Sheri Dawn*

It takes 20 years to build a reputation and five minutes to ruin it.
If you think about that, you'll do things differently.
— Warren Buffett

Seemingly inconsequential actions in the past can have radical effects on the future.
  – Debbi Shaffer

What we think, or what we know, or what we believe is,
in the end, of little consequence. The only consequence is what we do.
—John Ruskin

Don't think about what can happen in a month. Don't think about what can happen in a year.

Just focus on the 24 hours in front of you and do what you can to get closer to where you want to be.

(Unknown)

One of the most beautiful qualities of true friendship is
to understand and to be understood.
— *Lucius Annaeus Seneca*

Motivation doesn't come from waiting, motivation is caused by action.
  – *Garth Delikan*

Try to be a rainbow in someone's cloud.
— *Maya Angelou*

Whether you believe you can, or believe you can't, you're probably right.
  – *Henry Ford*

Better to ask a question and appear a fool for a minute
than be a fool for the rest of your life.
— Confucius

A person who has never made a mistake has never tried something new.
  – *Albert Einstein*

Human beings, by changing the inner attitudes of their minds,
can change the outer aspects of their lives.
— *William James*

You will never always be motivated. You have to learn to be disciplined.
  — Gymaholic

Lack of preparation on your part does not constitute a crisis on mine.
(Unknown)

WHAT I AM

I'm a neutral and independent advisor to my Executive, who enables the day-to-day management routines that enhance the effectiveness of my boss, and the organisation as a whole. I operate as a business manager in my own right – and I am an integral part of the management team. Moreover, I strive to demonstrate leadership qualities and align my behaviours to this goal accordingly. I am not a business partner as I sit in the core of the business; and I am not an optional extra – my role is mandatory to the success of my Executive. I work in the space of management, allowing my boss to focus on the bigger aspects of leadership.

© Adam Fidler, 2016

Not my circus, not my monkeys.
(Unknown)

Don't raise your voice, improve your argument.
  — Archbishop Desmond Tutu

You'll never change your life until you change something you do daily.
The secret of your success is found in your daily routine.

(Unknown)

Become an indispensable strategic asset now and in the future.
   — Joan Burge

Great minds discuss ideas; average minds discuss events; small minds discuss people.
— *Henry Thomas Buckle*

You can't start the next chapter of your life if you keep re-reading the last one.
(Unknown)

Clients do not come first. Employees come first.
If you take care of your employees first they will take care of the clients.
— *Sir Richard Branson*

A waterfall always begins with a drop of water.

— *The movie "Power of One"*

Option A is not available, so let's kick the shit out of option B.
— *Sheryl Sandberg*

Your value does not decrease based on someone's inability to see your worth.
   (Unknown)

Tact is the ability to tell someone to go to hell
in such a way that they look forward to the trip.
— *Winston Churchill*

If an Executive Assistant wants to really be strategic and be a business partner, she needs to get into that executive's world ... she needs to go from doing tasks, to thinking strategically, and understanding the business the way an executive understands the business.

– Jan Jones

Always be yourself, express yourself, have faith in yourself,
do not go out and look for a successful personality and duplicate it.

— Bruce Lee

If you can dream it, you can do it.
— *Walt Disney*

Action is the foundational key to all success.
— *Pablo Picasso*

Tell me and I will forget, show me and I will remember, involve me and I will learn.
— *Benjamin Franklin*

When people show you who they are, believe them the first time.
— *Maya Angelou*

Be the change you wish to see in the world.
    – Mahatma Gandhi

Strive not to be a success, but rather to be of value.
— *Albert Einstein*

You get in life what you have the courage to ask for.
    — Oprah Winfrey

Yesterday I was clever, so I wanted to change the world.
Today I am wise, so I am changing myself.
— *Rumi*

Be so good they can't ignore you.
    — Steve Martin

Time is the coin of your life. It is the only coin you have, and only you can determine
how it will be spent. Be careful lest you let other people spend it for you.
— *Carl Sandburg*

You may not know where you are, and God may know where you are...

...but if your Assistant doesn't know where you are, you'd better be on good terms with God.

(Unknown)

This role is one that will continue to change year on year, and to be successful at it you need a positive attitude, willingness to learn and to develop constantly.

— Victoria Darragh

The grass isn't always greener on the other side. It's green where you water it.
(Unknown)

Never underestimate your talent to initiate the power
in creating your personal mandate.
— *Michele Thwaits*

Colours, like features, follow the changes of emotions.
    – Pablo Picasso

Don't feel guilty about being out of the office to attend a program or conference
that will make you better equipped, faster, smarter and sharper.

— Joan Burge

Write it on your heart that every day is the best day in the year.
— *Ralph Waldo Emerson*

PAs beat Artificial Intelligence aids because of the emotional support they give, as well as insight into nuances and prioritising the ever-increasing deluge of information.

— Angela Mortimer

The grass is not greener on the other side, it's just different grass.
  — Rhonda Scharf

If you think you're too small to have an impact,
try going to bed with a mosquito in the room.
— *Dame Anita Roddick*

I disagree with what you say but I will defend to the death your right to say it.
  — *Voltaire*

What lies behind us and what lies before us
are tiny matters compared to what lies within us.
— *Ralph Waldo Emerson*

This above all: to thine own self be true
And it must follow, as the night the day
Thou canst not then be false to any man

– William Shakespeare

If you believe that a set of procedures can replace you,
you're not adding enough value to your company.
— *Julie Perrine*

You don't need a reason to help people.
(Unknown)

Awesome things happen when you find your voice
to speak up about the things that matter.
— *Bonnie Low Kramen*

You don't get what you deserve, you get what you negotiate.
  – *Chester Karrass*

You are valuable just because you exist. Not because of what you do or what you have done, but simply because you are.

— *Max Lucado*

If you aren't getting answers, ask better questions.
(Unknown)

The trouble with doing something right the first time
is that no one appreciates how difficult it was.
— *Walter J West*

The time is always right to do what is right.
— *Martin Luther King Jr*

Your reputation is more important than your paycheck,
and your integrity is worth more than you career.
— *Ryan Freitas*

Laugh as much as you breathe and love as long as you live.
(Unknown)

If you can't fly, then run, if you can't run then walk, if you can't walk then crawl,
but whatever you do you have to keep moving forward.
— *Martin Luther King Jr*

Communication creates partnerships. We are here to assist you, but we can't make your life for you and we can't help you with things that we don't know. And you always have to remember to take care of you first and foremost. Because when you stop taking care of yourself, you get out of balance and you really forget how to take care of others.

– Jada Pinkett Smith

Peace: it doesn't mean to be in a place where there is no noise, trouble or hard work. It means to be in the midst of those things and still be calm in your heart.

(Unknown)

Don't think outside the box. Think like there is no box.
(Unknown)

Carry out random acts of kindness, with no expectation of reward,
safe in the knowledge that one day someone might do the same for you.
— *Princess Diana*

You don't build a business, you build people and then people build the business.
 – *Zig Zigler*

Never minimise your work or the place you are within your knowledge.
Just know that it is a stage in your development.
– *Donna Gilliland*

The single biggest problem in communication is the illusion that it has taken place.
— *George Bernard Shaw*

One of the greatest regrets in life is not taking action and failing,
but failing to take action.
— *Nick Fewings*

If it's important to you, you'll find a way. If not, you'll find an excuse.
(Unknown)

The value that an Assistant delivers is in direct proportion
to the amount of burden they lessen for hours.
— Nick Fewings

Do not judge my story by the chapter you walked in on.
(Unknown)

Being humble means recognising we are not on earth to see how important we can become, but to see how much difference we can make in the lives of others.

– Gordon B Hinckley

Take ownership of your job and elevate it without being asked and without asking. Do what's best for your work and your company's success. Earn a reputation for innovation and excellence in every aspect of what you do. That will only increase the freedom you are given, not jeopardize it.

– Darla Barrett

Start by doing what's necessary, then do what's possible;
and suddenly you are doing the impossible.
— *Francis of Assisi*

The key is not to prioritise what's on your schedule, but to schedule your priorities.
— *Steve Covey*

Never understand the power of a small group of committed people
to change the world. In fact, it is the only thing that ever has.
— *Margaret Mead, Anthopologist*

Success is not final; failure is not fatal. It is the courage to continue that counts.
  — *Winston Churchill*

A great attitude becomes a great mood, which becomes a great day,
which becomes a great year, which becomes a great life.
(Unknown)

Try not to become a person of success. Rather become a person of value.
  — *Albert Einstein*

What you get by achieving your goals is not as important as
what you become by achieving your goals.
— Henry David Thoreau

Done is better than perfect.
 – Mark Zuckerberg

My mission in life is not merely to survive, but to thrive;
and to do so with some passion, some compassion, some humour and some style.

— Maya Angelou

Adopt the pace of nature: her secret is patience.
  — *Ralph Waldo Emerson*

How wonderful it is that nobody need wait a single moment
before starting to improve the world.
— *Anne Frank*

No-one lives long enough to learn everything they need to learn starting from scratch. To be successful, we absolutely, positively have to find people who have already paid the price to learn the things that we need to learn to achieve our goals.

– Brian Tracy

It takes courage to grow up and become who you really are.

— *e.e. cummings*

Knowing others is wisdom, knowing yourself is Enlightenment.
   — Lao Tzu

Our deepest fear is not that we are inadequate.
Our deepest fear is that we are powerful beyond measure.
— *Marianne Williamson*

You miss 100% of the shots you don't take.
    — *Wayne Gretzky*

We are one profession, with one voice
and we are changing peoples' lives one person at a time.
— *Lucy Brazier*

Have an attitude of gratitude.
　　 — *Kemetia Foley*

If it's your job to eat a frog, it's best to do it first thing in the morning.
And If it's your job to eat two frogs, it's best to eat the biggest one first.

— Mark Twain

The true sign of intelligence is not knowledge but imagination.
   – *Albert Einstein*

87% of employers surveyed believe
they could not do their job as effectively without their Assistant.
— *Hays research 2015*

If you don't like change, you are going to like irrelevance even less.
  – *General Eric Shinseki*

We need to be constantly evolving to survive
and the excellence needs to come from YOU!
— *Lucy Brazier*

Twenty years from now you will be more disappointed by the things that you didn't do than by the ones you did do.

So throw off the bowlines. Sail away from the safe harbour. Catch the trade winds in your sails.

Explore. Dream. Discover.

– Mark Twain

The secret of change is to focus all of your energy,
not on fighting the old, but on building the new.
— *Dan Millman*

"No" is a complete sentence.
— *Susie Barron Stubley*

Most Assistants have amazing talents and competencies that are
not being used to anything like their full potential.
— *Susie Barron Stubley*

Today is the tomorrow you worried about yesterday and all is well.
— *Duncan Brazier*

Point out my mistakes; you've lost me that instant.
Help me overcome them; you've won me for life.
—*Jonathan Sprinkles*

They are not the expert at being the Assistant, you are!
– Lucy Brazier

If an Assistant can figure out how to scratch their manager's itch
and ease their pain, they will never be unemployed.
— *Bonnie Low Kramen*

Formal education will make you a living; self-education will make you a fortune.
  — *Jim Rohn*

A journey of a thousand miles must begin with a single step.

— Lao Tzu

Life begins at 90.
   – Sonia Vanular, Founder of EUMA at 95

Don't doubt your own skillset. You may have additional skills that a company has never seen before, and will be worth their weight in gold to that organisation – don't be afraid to show them off and speak up!
– *Victoria Darragh*

Helen is my memory. She travels the world with me, is delightful to have around, and is extremely adaptable and sociable wherever we find ourselves. With so much going on with my mind, having an extra memory is important. Before I ask her to do something, she can read my mind and know what it is I am thinking before I ask.

– Richard Branson (when asked about his Assistant)

Imagine a world where people wake up inspired to go to work.
— *Simon Sinek*

Shut the Duck Up!
 — Susie Barron Stubley (on how to deal with negative voices in your head)

Knowledgeable Assistants are more than a productivity asset:
They're reverse mentors, using their experience to teach new executives
how people are expected to behave at that level in the organization.
— *Melba Duncan*

Treat others as you would like to be treated.
(Unknown)

If a problem is fixable, if a situation is such that you can do something about it,
then there is no need to worry. If it's not fixable, then there is no help in worrying.
There is no benefit in worrying whatsoever.
— *The Dalai Lama*

And so the adventure begins...
(Unknown)

Set priorities for your goals. A major part of successful living lies in the ability to put first things first. Indeed, the reason most major goals are not achieved is that we spend our time doing second things first.

(Unknown)

It's not who you think you are that holds you back, it's who you think you are not.
— *Lucy Brazier*

Two critical factors determine how well a manager utilizes an Assistant. The first is the executive's willingness to delegate pieces of his or her workload to the Assistant. The second is the Assistant's willingness to stretch beyond his or her comfort zone to assume new responsibilities.

— *Melba Duncan*

What matters most is how you see yourself.
  – *Lucy Brazier*

Words are very important to how you can change your beliefs; a person with
a fixed mindset might say "I can't do that" or "I'm not good at maths" etc.
but a person with a growth mindset would add a very important word
to the end of those sentences and that is – "yet"!

– *Sue France*

I know that at this very moment, there is someone, somewhere, right now working late on a proposal or spreadsheet or presentation and quite possibly in tears. This hurts me to the core. I don't want anyone to feel powerless or struggle with their documents, especially when they have the tools they need to deliver results in less time. I want admins to master these tools so that they can focus on what matters most, supporting their team and delivering results fast, not fighting with technology.

– Vickie Sokol Evans

In today's competitive marketplace and at the pace this profession is changing,
if you do not continually enhance your skills, build new ones,
and have a strategy for your career, you will get left in the dust.
— Joan Burge

The best way to find yourself is to lose yourself in the service of others.
– Gandhi

I have this image of this enormous group of women across the world as a sleeping giant, that when awakened to the beauty of speaking up and collaborating with one another, will change the world in glorious ways.

— *Bonnie Low Kramen*

How will you serve your profession?
— *Lucy Brazier*

The pathway itself isn't important, what matters is, that the administrative professional has chosen for themselves what that pathway is to be, and takes responsibility for their own professional development opportunities to achieve it.

– Eth Lloyd

You are not a tree! If you don't like where you are, uproot yourself and leave!
 — *Anel Martin*

When used correctly, technology can change the way you work
and ultimately your life. And when I hear this firsthand from my students,
I'm even more inspired and motivated to continue my mission.
— *Vickie Sokol Evans*

Make yourself happy, because you can!
    – *Cathy Harris*

One of the best things you can do for your executive is to fill the gap. Know your manager's strengths and limitations so well that you set him/her up for success by utilizing your strengths to fill the gap in one of their areas of weakness.

– Peggy Vasquez

I am a professional, I am intentional
I am backstage producing award winning executives
I am a producer of life changing events
I am a starter, I am a finisher
I am strongest in my being; I am a professional

– Florence Katono

It's what you learn after you know it all that counts.
—*John Wooden*

Don't ever underestimate the impact that you may have on someone else's life.
   (Unknown)

Respond to every call that excites your spirit.
— *Rumi*

When you get, give; when you learn, teach.
— *Maya Angelou*

Nobody said the world was fair, they only said it was round.
(Unknown)

You've always had the power my dear, you just had to learn it for yourself.
— *The Wizard of Oz*

There are only two days in the year that nothing can be done. One is called yesterday and the other is called tomorrow.

So today is the right day to love, believe, do, and mostly, live.

– The Dalai Lama

Executive Secretary
MAGAZINE

#OneProfessionOneVoice

www.executivesecretary.com

CPSIA information can be obtained
at www.ICGtesting.com
Printed in the USA
LVOW11*1208100917
548118LV00006BA/102/P